out of the bonecage singing

carla martin-wood

THE PINK PETTICOAT PRESS
Not your grandmother's poetry

With much love

for my son

Zachary Arthur Wood

in whom I am well pleased

The most beautiful experience we can have is the mysterious. It is the fundamental emotion which stands at the cradle of true art and true science. Whoever does not know it and can no longer wonder, no longer marvel, is as good as dead, and his eyes are dimmed.

Albert Einstein

****

Energy cannot be created or destroyed;
it can only be changed from one form to another.

Albert Einstein

From the author

A number of gracious and accomplished poet friends offered to contribute the introduction to this little book. However, I wanted to write an introduction myself this time, not to elucidate the poems – for interpretation is the province of each reader – but to talk about the source of this collection, which began its journey when I was only seven.

Only my most trusted friends have heard this story – and none of my family. However, I'm an old lady now, and I don't worry about what people think anymore.

I had chronic asthma, and in 1953, there were no great medicines to help me. On this particular occasion, the condition was coupled with a bad infection. I became unconscious, and anticipating the worst, the doctor stayed the night in my grandparents' modest home.

Being a stubborn child, I fooled them all. My fever broke, the doctor departed, and I lay there in a deep sleep till dawn, when I was wakened by April morning light pouring through the windows.

All I could think about was escaping into that sunlight. I had been sick for so long, and I needed the light. I knew my grandparents would never allow me to go out – but they were asleep and would be none the wiser if I simply went out on my own.

My legs were shaking from weakness – I vividly remember that morning and everything about it, from trembling body to sharply acute senses, as I wrapped a blanket around myself and made my way down Grandmother's back steps.

I recall how mud squished between my toes, and the way drops of a predawn rain clung to the yellow green leaves. Birdsong. Everything was shiny and so new. Now when I remember that morning, Frost's *Nothing Gold Can Stay* immediately comes to mind. There was a light, chill wind, and I remember drawing the blanket close around me. But mostly, I remember something that changed me, shaped my belief system, and made me a poet who would spend a lifetime trying to explain impossible things.

I was suddenly out of my body – it was as though I just slipped out of this bonecage while no one was looking – just as I had sneaked out of the house while my grandparents slept.

I could see myself below for a second, but then I was quickly everywhere at once. Inside a bird where I felt the shudder of its wings against the cold; in every individual drop of rain that trembled on the edges of newly formed spring leaves; then, in the leaves themselves – in the air – everywhere, and all at the same instant.

Remarkably, it was completely familiar to me. I was not frightened at all. I was comfortable. There was no pain anymore. I was weightless and aware that I was a sort of energy that could be in any "container" or completely free.

Then in all that excitement and freedom, I knew instinctively I was being asked to make a decision. I knew that I had the option to stay out there and participate in everything. I knew someone or something was giving me this choice.

I answered that I was so happy to be in a body again *this time*, even if it would never work right and would never be a very good body. I said I wished to stay. That answer did not come from the seven year old mind or body. It came from my spirit and was directed to its Maker, and it was very old.

Immediately, I was back in my body, and Papa was lifting me up in his arms and taking me back inside the warm house where bacon was cooking and my grandmother was not pleased with me.

After that day, I asked too many questions in church. I was constantly reprimanded for my odd beliefs. At seven, I was not equipped to explain what had happened to me – I still am not so equipped. Yet, I knew that these manmade religions had it all wrong. I knew the atheists had it wrong, too.

I would never look at nature the same way again – I was forever changed, for I knew that there is this oneness. And I knew there was an all-encompassing Love. I also knew there was more to me than ephemeral flesh and bone – that this form is just a vehicle.

From that April morning forward, I filled notebooks with poems. I had no choice. I was inundated by words, as though they had all flooded in while I was floating out there, inhabiting raindrops and sparrows.

A Jesuit friend once told me that we go through thousands of deaths and resurrections during our lives: abandonments, deaths of ideals, deaths of relationships, actual deaths of those dear to us. During my time here, I have most certainly experienced those losses – and they are true deaths, whether the death of a cherished belief in someone, the death of a mind, or the actual demise of a person – even our faith. And we mourn and try to move on.

In explaining the world, we are confined to three dimensions. Only Einstein had a tenuous grasp on the space-time continuum – the mortal mind deals in the concrete. We must make sense of what we see and experience, or there is chaos.

Therefore, we very naturally include a *place* where we can feel comfortable that our loved ones go when they cross over from this life. Some call it heaven, others, paradise. The more pessimistic include hell, limbo, purgatory. Westerners don't easily consider that the spirit's destination may not be a place, but a *state of being*. Moreover, that this may be just a pit stop on the way to another incarnation.

I have come to call that state of being "afterwhere" – and while I certainly lay no claim to answers, that fleeting event when I was a child colors these poems, which encompass the deaths, small and large, that we encounter in this lifetime, our losses, our reactions, the natural world that mitigates our suffering, and contemplation of what it all may mean.

This book is about the mortal and immortal in us. It's my personal path, and I don't ask that you accept what I believe or even believe the backstory. These poems are my way of thanking the Universe for the strange journey gifted to me at the age of seven, wrapped in a blanket, standing in a backyard that smelled of earth and rain, mud squishing up between my toes. It is my way of giving thanks for how that experience shaped me into a poet.

I hope you find something of beauty here.

Carla Martin-Wood
January, 2014

Poems

Poems

Deception

In the fireflied childhood of my life
wildwood where I ran feral and unfettered
in the white pearl morningworld
I gloried in each liliaceous sky
in borning rays of rising sun
unwary of what comes
that flesh declines, and in the deepnight
even brightest stars refuse to shine
their light invisible to eyes
whose sweetest joy has soured to sorrow
that what is made this day in paradise
can be destroyed tomorrow and
buried close beneath the newborn face
so graceless and impatient wait
void-eyed skull and polished bone
that twilight comes, the strongest fail
and quite alone we finally bed down
a deathwatch of our ghostly forebears
gathered round to mock
or that the blackrobed cart
thunders close behind
its ominous vibrations jar
grind spirit, mind and joints
sick secret hidden as an appleworm
in swaddling clothes of every foundling babe
and through soulcaverns, death howls
hungry as the owl that seeks its prey
or that we all must fall to ash someday.

October song

The wind goes picking apples, and they fall
she doesn't care to choose by cultivar
the Granny Smith, Delicious, Delrouval
all find their way to press or canning jar

The wind goes picking apples, and they fall
regardless of estate or pedigree
befreckled, bruised, gourmet, she gathers all
and none escapes her reaping that I see

Forget her sweet, flirtatious dance in May
through heavy-honeyed blossoms on each limb
her whispered breezes that began the play
grow colder with her final harvest hymn

We line her greedy baskets, one and all
the wind goes picking apples, and we fall.

First

Down paths worn bare
by winter boots
we found a woodland
awash in blooms
burdened with April
and wild with spring
alive with hum of bees
and wings
gossamer and white
they fluttered by
all one with blossomed trees
in heavy-honeyed prophecy
of fruit that could not be

there on the bridge
he enfolded me
as though I were a thing
of petals made and spring
that merest breath
might dissipate
and scatter to the winds
forever lost
and there we kissed
first, last
and not again

for fate let slip
the fragile string
that held us bound
to love stillborn
that breathed but once
and left our worlds
forlorn.

Endings

Intoxicating hours spent with you
the Beaujolais nouvelle, the burning leaves
the surface of the lake so still and blue
as autumn fields displayed their golden sheaves

We watched the sunset paint a masterpiece
insinuated endings in the glow
of scarlet streaks and elegant cerise
it tinctured fading skies with indigo

Your silhouette's embedded in my mind
against November's bright kaleidoscope
the veil that lifted quickly and unkind
revealed the bleak futility of hope

And I remember standing on the edge
one foot in heaven, one just off the ledge.

Love in the space-time continuum

If time is just a construct we impose
to organize a tolerable view
when everything is happening at once
and present, past and future are the same

then spring Monets our ancient woodland still
daubs pinks and purples gingerly among
the dogwood blossoms luminous and pale
that float like ghosts when twilight takes the skies

and he and I walk through that April glade
eternally first lovers, always young
where juice and jubilation are the call
of every piper in the verdant wood

and while we dance to those immortal tunes
then elsewhere must love stumble, fall and die.

Witness

I can testify that you lived
to the end of the rhyme
to the final iamb
to the shadows of the couplet
we formed on your bed
in a room where the only sound
was our breathing as one
where the pools of your eyes
drew me down
your mouth an animal seeking refuge
your soul grown dark like moss
hidden between the lilies of my breasts
so that Hunter Death lost
his quarry for a moment
seeing only one lying there
until night dropped
below the skyline like a stone
and morning came at last
the small, grey sparrows of our lives
fallen to earth unnoticed.

Mourning

Sudden was your leaving
under a sunless sky
without good-bye
or a note on your pillow
before the waking world
made breakfast
or smoked its first cigarette

Spirit gone
you fly free
leave me naked among thorns
disarmed
half of myself
stranger
in an ordinary land
missing your voice
that spoke mysterious
a language of crows
missing the wine
forbidden
rare and spilled like blood
upon white linen

I am stranded
wishing to refute
the gravity that holds me
to this world
without contrast
flat
without depth or height
without salt

No summoning
invokes you
there is no patch
to counter this addiction

I cannot breathe

My sacred dark
my fallen angel
my broken wing.

The space between

Ley lines connect us
like great mountains
or pyramids
or those inexplicable drawings
only visible from great heights
invisibly tethered
each to each
we defy space
time

where
ever you are
when
ever I am
and if I shift in sleep
I know you
grow restless
at the other end
and wake
I quake
when you tremble
aspens

ash and wind
do not dissolve
nor does earth hide
darkwinged angel
on the other side of after
I sense you there
you sense me here
pulling
pulling.

Mabon

Breath of her breath
incense rising
from leafy forest floor
smoke permeates crisp air
fists beat skin drums
we pour libations
of water and sweet wine
adorn her altar
with fruit and grain
celebrate this holy season
fires of summer die
by chant and dance
we invoke and bless her
thank her for her bounty
praise her beauty
burning now in every tree

Goddess harvestclad
embered ambers
umbers and scarlet
wheel of the year turns
cold as stone toward winter
earthsleep comes soon
with its silent longing for snow
black limbs silhouette
against grey sky
all is chiaroscuro for a time
comatose world dreams
spring to follow
nothing is shallow
all is hallowed
hollow hammer of flickers
in the distance.

Consecration

Swallows rise
bloom into grey skies
then scatter
above a world lit
by autumn lanterns dangled
through tangles of scarlet vines
and blackened branches

I sit atop this rock at Morgan's Steep
its face a sculpture wind and water worn
and lay aside my sketchbook

charcoal cannot replicate
the riotous palette below
Cumberland Plateau unfurled
patchwork splendor
a quilt Grandmother might have stitched
to comfort me

in fact, I find myself inclined
within my rebel pagan mind
to believe that she did
and that she watches
from her home in afterwhere
knowing how I love it here
which was to her a sin
but freed from bone and skin
perhaps she understands
and loves me still

I watch with eyes half-closed
as autumn Van Goghs the canvas
insane with sorrel
mad with goldenrod

crazed by haystacks and fields
mown or harvested
all kindled on November's pyre

the old year consecrates the ash to evening
with her cold and starry night
she calls us home
to human warmth before the fire
to the hallowed, transient presence
of each other.

Samhain

How many years I waded shallows
shrouded in myth this holy day
when bonfires burn on every hill
and the veil strains to such thin membrane
that natives of the other realm
can breach the border

How long I failed to embrace
the ancient masterpiece over which
the modern world has painted in broad strokes
a fairytale to cover the old truth
made it a child's day of begging for sweets
with masks to camouflage

Today my life moves forward
after so long an illness
trembling legs navigate
gardens that had been closed to me
as Eden was to Eve
today, when my heart rejoices
at this bluesky morning
at rambunctious squirrels
that spiral up bright birches
chipmunks that leap startled
at the noise of brittle leaves
and my old gypsy spirit resurrects
bones dance to birdsong
today, when I harvest happiness
find again the treasure
in common light and simple stone
when I delight
to earth's pulse beneath bare feet
and melodies of water underground

Now that cobblestoned rumble
as the old cart draws near
wheels ominous
and I know what shadow works to spoil
the happy canvas that I paint at last
the presence of my grandmother
her frost-hung breath on my neck
she who never knew a day of joy
whispers that I cannot walk
to spare myself the pain
tells me shelter behind four walls
whispers: *die*
I talk to her out loud, tell her

> *Sleep at last, poor woman*
> *find solace in your darkness*
> *I am not coming to you yet*
> *but when I do*
> *I shall come dancing*
> *I shall bring poppies and red wine*
> *I shall be accompanied by birds*
> *and tokens from the greenworld*
> *laughter, song*
> *and all those things that frightened you.*

Tabula rasa

The blue hour
purple dark
glower of clouds
hung low
moon hides and seeks
me at my window
in Earl Grey comfort
I watch
as snow begins
a slow descent
and Bach
so softly
takes it all away

Bullet hole souvenir
mars my perfect window
last year
I watched
the parking lot below
burst into gunfire
sirens
yellow tape
blood pooled dark
bodies
zipped without ceremony
into bags
anonymous refuse

First light
they washed the blood away
casual as a man
might hose grass clippings
from his driveway

---

blood
black now and gummy
blasted by the spray
flowed pink and foamy
into the gutter
except for a gory footprint
some cop left behind
I walked around it for weeks
avoided that side of the street

Now this great eraser
makes it all white
restores the innocence
removes the stain
cleanses
so spring can come
with its petals
pollen will drift
cover the lot
where cars will park
and children play again

When we die
I believe
it's neither dark nor angels
that we see
not dear familiar faces
nor the devils we deserve
only the white
that takes it all away.

The suicide

I am not Lizzie lying here
sighing here drifting
in this float of flowers
petal coins soft upon eyes
that cannot unsee
I am no Ophelia

and not a mermaid
once knife-walking land lover
now fishtailed again
and broken
Hamlet-hearted sister
who could not do
what should be done
tangle-haired with jingle shells
awash in weedy brine
she waits for the quick dissolve
into a foam finale

nothing so romantic
no legend am I

only a woman mortal
soul heavy, bone weary
stone dropped into the chest for ballast
lured by the cold clean
sea-sky emptiness
dark hearts that once beat
to my rhythm
remembered now, leaden
weights they hold me
motionless save for waves
of Mother who rocks me to and fro

to a sadsong lullaby of scavengers
as I let it all go at last
into the salty void

before the riptide breaks me tears me
before another net ensnares me.

Joe Bar

Joe Bar is gone
four walls with no ceiling
to deter dreams
the four of us brought there
when we were eager
students of the world
who dissected every lecture
over Joe's dark ale
or read our poems
at the piano bar
looking out at kaleidoscope trees
third Thursday afternoon each November
the Beaujolais not nearly
as nouveau as we
damned children
of a Left Bank delusion
stuck in a steel town
sad and grey, no exit

Brad is gone
who made a pilgrimage to Rome
drank a toast to Keats for me
brought flowers for his grave
wrapped in a poem I wrote
because he knew I'd never make the trip
close-as-any-brother Brad
lean and strong and beautiful TA
strutting cocky before the class
cigarette a permanent accessory
tucked beneath the upper lip
don't ask, don't tell, closeted
in those days, but with me
hanging on his arm and every word
no one guessed his secret

till AIDS claimed him
when it barely had a name

Linda is gone
blonde and laughing
best friend pretender
who shacked up with the husband
of a woman who was dying
and slept her way
through halls of academia
dead by her own bloody hand
in a motel room
somewhere upstate

Marcus is gone
who aced Chaucer
and axed debate opponents
but flunked elementary ethics
bright-eyed politico
ark of our hopes
gone to rot in some prison
for malfeasance
if gold ruste, what shall iren do?

Joo Dai Is gone
and where shall they go now
the ghosts of who we were
our beloved dart board gone long ago
the million holes around a pristine bull's-eye
pock-marked wainscoting that saw the best in us
replaced by glitter-embedded stucco
some redneck's design
intended to mimic heaven
Steinway kept to play a Pied Piper tune
for this newly opened inner city church
zealots who would have sent us all to hell
as though we couldn't find the way
ourselves.

Plea to autumn

Burn me, Autumn!

Blind me with your glory
for what is left to see
when you are gone

Dazzle my last vision
with your incandescence
russet red and golden

See how your presence
trembles through these limbs
with your slightest breath
how color scintillates

Incinerate me
on a pyre
fire fragranced
by your leaves
piled high in every lane

Scatter my ashes
on the brisk wings
of your waking winds

Lay me gentle
across the lap of April
to feed new life
that I, too, may shine
among your branches
upon your bright return.

Outcast in autumn

There is no greater sorrow than to recall in misery the time when we were happy.
– Dante Alighieri

I am not happy
that the long slant of October light
triggers these memories of you
nor that the bright trail up the mountain
recalls how you followed me so closely
that you stepped on the heels of my boots
leaving scuff marks like dark bruises

I find no joy
that the inseparable separates
in a caesura between words
in a flash that falls between shadows
the infinitesimal silence between the tick of seconds
nor that your dash into the woods
to chase a late Monarch through burning maples
is pressed into my mind like dried leaves between wax paper
and Crayola'd cards and photographs
are eternal afterimages that cannot be erased
when I close my eyes to sleep

I am not pleased
that these things embed themselves into my mind
in this my own autumn, as skies grow dark
a line of demarcation drawn between us
that cannot be breached

I was not prepared
for there was neither sign nor harbinger nor omen
to prophecy a time when you would leave
and I would stand at Hades' door
that Cerberus guarded passage
alone and with no papers
winter on the wind.

The diagnosis

In old cartoons
the crazy coyote
raced through the desert
right off an impossible cliff
kept on running
doing just fine
till he looked down
and gravity
sent him plummeting

It was that way
with Papa
that wiley old man
who mowed his own lawn
tended his garden
swung great-grandkids high
danced jigs
walked to church
leaning on his blackthorn shillelagh
uttered the occasional groan or expletive
when he thought no one in earshot
but hell, he was nearing seventy

Then one afternoon
he acknowledged the pain
was a bit worse
and shocked by his admission
Grandmother rushed him
to the ER

Prostate cancer
metastatic
riddled his bones
the doctor half-joked

How did you get here, man?
See? The x-rays show you have no pelvis
he called in a covey of cronies
showed off his find
the miracle man
who walked and danced and strutted
with no visible support

They rolled him out to the parking lot
in a wheelchair
assured him this was better
than the agony of walking
sent him home
where he went to bed
didn't get up

Papa
who lived on his own
as a child
taught himself to read
survived a mining disaster
that crushed his legs
taught himself to walk again
when doctors said *No*
kicked morphine cold turkey
now he was outnumbered
chased right off the cliff
by this flock of doomsayers
machines that taunted
beep beep cancer beep beep
beep beep cancer beep beep
and with the full weight of
this Acme of medicine
pressed relentlessly upon him

Papa looked down.

Papa's finale

Always a dancer at heart
from the swing in your step
to the occasional jig
to amuse or embarrass us

Then cancer called the tune
and left you still

That night we huddled around the old table
every dysfunctional child
another mute self-involved meal
but served with a darker silence
an individual grief

Then stillness shattered

Your old blackthorn walking stick
leaned against the hearth
useless these three years

We startled when we heard it
rap against the wall
a sharp tapping
and something
vibrations of the house
passing traffic
caused it to stand upright
dance in quick staccato
then fall back again

Skittish laughter all round
disbelief smart remarks
but I knew

You were dancing
down the Milky Way
strutting like a sailor on leave
doing your mad Irish jig
from the Moon
to the rings of Saturn
a Texas reel at the edge of Time
a wild Tennessee clog
a crazy Cajun two-step
straight into the arms of God.

Skydiver

In your 51-year freefall
you feared nothing but gravity
whatever held you down, fenced you in, made you stop

never once considered that impactful moment
when birdboned body meets stone
always knew an updraft would save you
relied on the reprieve of air currents
you could ride awhile

floated arms out, waiting for evening magic
when warm air from the valley
buoyed you upward into the sunset

lifted effortless
through Maxfield Parrish clouds
nothing tugged at you
called you back
from the edge of the atmosphere

then at night, silvered and soaring, light as ether
I never doubted you
fed pearls to the moon till it grew full
then lit the stars
like votives in the sky

came the day downdrafts betrayed you
how surprised you must have been
when earth opened her arms.

Bedside, pianissimo

Last days
having sung
your wild song
capriccio
the diminuendo began
to its breathless
conclusion
I watched life perch
fermata
on frail rib staves
then a sudden, final flutter
teased against walls
and bonecage broken
it flew free
hearing otherwhere
perhaps
some whisper
of a prelude
leaving you empty
finale a dim echo
in the vaulted hall
and me wondering
if ever I would dance
again.

Essence
for my mother

This artifact from caverns of my youth
does not contain a djinn to bring you back
there is no carpet ride
twixt here and afterwhere
and yet there is
this journey of the mind

Saved forty years, this bottle
sticky with a yellow residue
that I refuse to clean
because a bit of you lingers still
just below the cap
this precious reliquary
holds a partial fingerprint
your sacred DNA

The label with its ancient faded rose
I hold to my lips
a redolence of vanilla and sweet musk
the scent of you envelopes
like a spell

Years fall away and I see you
stop strangers in their tracks
to watch a flame-haired woman
skin pale, cheeks radiant
she makes angels with her daughter in the snow
the tintinnabulation of their laughter
floats upward teasing heaven

I never thought to borrow it
this fragranced treasure
at first, I was a child

then older thought it wasn't hip
and didn't work with my granola youth

I catch a mirrored glimpse
of who I am today
silver-haired, old
with lines no laughter ever made
yet know I need a mother
more than my child-self ever did
I taste the salty truth
and claim my legacy
twist the cap
plunge the dropper in
press upon my throat
one priceless drop.

.

Love song for my brother

Edwin Ross Martin
May 30, 1954-January 7, 2010

Strangers in the nest, we were
unlike the other two
we shared Mother's milk
white skin, fine bones
it bound us for a time
born after me
I watched over you
till things changed
malignant childhood
Mother's toxic men and
Halloween when you were twelve
LSD on your candy
bad trick
bad trip
to the hospital
flashbacks
and bit by bit
superimposed
upon my face you saw
the Mother you abhorred
on yours, I saw
the Mother I adored
and the violence began
until my fear of you
bound up the love

Birmingham 1998
late summer concert
picnic blanket
chardonnay and Vivaldi
with a friend
till you appeared
shining in white linen

dark glasses
hair black as a crow's wing
your long-legged stride
stunned the provincials
into silence
damaged and damned
sinuous you descended
elegant among olive branches

We talked
and your red-brown eyes
flashed like Mother's
for a moment
I glimpsed
my tortured brother
chained within

You called
two weeks before you died
begged me to pick up
but I made myself stone
deaf, remembered loving you
was losing myself
in deep water
you were sucked under
hands reaching for help
but at my touch
you dragged me down
and I struggled
kicked hard
to escape

Three years gone now
I regret
at what expense
I saved myself

remember
how you walked away
beneath my window
rejected
shattering my heart
like no one else
in that rumpled tweed
shoulders hunched
head down
rain on your hair
like diamonds.

Desolation
(on the death of my brother)

That day starlings rushed forth
from the barn
into a flood of light
wings beat bleak air
sounded the alarm
and I woke
to a world of crows and carrion
mind fog-filled, grey
I walked the lake's edge
where weeds flattened
making patterns
petroglyphs on water
indecipherable
stepped into shallows
dappled in shadows
dark
dark
to the bottom
where mud tried to swallow
my bare feet
held me fast
religion failed
fruit fell
worm riddled
unripe
beat of my pulse
a percussive regret
broken
broken
each memory
large to minute
molten swords
quenched in blood

each chance
at reconciliation
shattered
shattered
lost.

Dirge in the key of Alzheimer's

In your thirties
four times you failed
at suicide
now we must bear witness
to the neverending end of you
as things that matter turn to grey
as lights wink out

memory / motivation / desire
address / phone number / username / password
Heaney / Bach / seven languages
the book you were writing
our letters
friends / family / cats
and me

what made you
laugh
what made you
sad
what made you
dissolves

thoughts scatter like startled birds
the fingerprint of your mind burns away
we mourn you
cell by cell

the perfect suicide
living to watch bewildered
your perpetual funeral
mirrored in the eyes
of those who dare to stay.

Legacy

This poem is for Great Aunt Myrtle
gypsy-wild woman
Black Irish crazy
feral and fabulous
with her bold dark eyes
and her untamed ways
and her spirit savage and strange
that called her out
into moonlit fields
the night she ran away
from the quiet farm
to join a Vaudeville troupe

and this is for that rampant rhythm
that rocked her blood
as she hoofed it across the stage
the forbidden cigarettes she smoked
the fires she stoked
the rules she broke
and the hearts

this is for streets she marched in bloomers
outrageous suffragette
still shouting
when they dragged her away
to jail cells that could not hold her

this is for the black-red roses
I would place on her grave
had the family not been too ashamed
to write her scandalous name in the Bible
or record where she was buried

---

this is for the woman I never met
never heard about
till I was thirty

this poem is for the breadcrumbs
she cast behind
as she danced
marking the path I followed
without knowing.

Feeding the bear

For Alana

Wall Street had its ceilings
our law firm had a glass floor
beneath which we could not fall
from grace and nothing above us
to which we might rise

it was from that limbo we fled
on autumn weekends
to mountains flamboyant
only two hours' distant
packing enough food and water
to get us through
a vegetarian apocalypse

we practiced healthy insanity
worked off our angst
fueled by granola
picnicked on hummus and raw veggies
apples stuffed with peanut butter
gulped handfuls of vitamins
and that dreadful Chinese tea you loved
hiked every trail
no matter how steep the incline
pushed one foot in front of another
let death take the hindmost

once we found ourselves
surrounded by deer
and a tiny fawn
they had no fear
even when we walked
between them
it was a shared innocence

and once we sat perfectly still
unbreathing
when a thud in the brush
shook the ground beneath us
from the smell, we knew
that old black grizzly
rangers warned us about
was scant yards away
it snorted, shuffled off
we laughed, boasted
that it would never touch us

now fragments of those days
strung on a thread too fragile
drift through my mind
as I try to sleep against the pain
of age, arthritis, raw nerves

and I remember
how you were not 40
when death lumbered into our camp
undetected
dragged you away screaming
to some uncharted afterwhere
and how beneath this moon
that throws long shadows
across my bedroom wall
your ashes are cast
owl feathers
across my fitful dreams.

Three days

And Jesus going up to Jerusalem took the twelve disciples apart in the way, and said unto them, Behold, we go up to Jerusalem; and the Son of man shall be betrayed unto the chief priests and unto the scribes, and they shall condemn him to death, and shall deliver him to the Gentiles to mock, and to scourge, and to crucify him: and the third day he shall rise again. – Matthew 20:17-19

I

Behind him
thirty silver coins
cast into the dust
and the tears of a woman
prison doors slam shut
thorns pierce tender flesh
cat-o-nine punishes
vinegar bites
joints tear
a sword pierces
till bonecage broken
the dove breaks free
and all is cool and dark
in this borrowed bed
pungent with the smell
of funeral spices
this tomb
where he can finally lie down

II

He is otherwhere
moon and stars
make a dance of light
sun rises pink and gold
on dogwood petals

glimmer of an afterworld
no burdens or borders
incense rises sweet
from the forest floor
butterflies scatter
laughter sings
children play
in a boundless meadow
maidens weave roses
in their hair
young men tattoo themselves
with red ochre
pour wine
make music and love
this is the Green Man's world
full of joy
full of juice
full of grace
sinless and simple
no need for stone-written laws
no politics with cross purposes
no betrayals
no chalice of blood
no reason to die

III

He revives
outside three women
speak to angels
his palms want to bleed again
soon he will go home
to solemn lilies
still waters
obligatory psalms
sung by the docile blest.

The lamb fell

The lamb fell
not knowing the destiny
of its fine wool

Nor that one strand would hold as anchor
to the others that formed
curls and loops encircling it
to spin the softest boucle

Nor that it was dyed
a sweet – yet assertive – pink
or that some said
it was shipped to Chez Ninon
to be fashioned into the navy-collared suit
following line-by-line orders
dictated by the House of Chanel

Nor that it would be fitted meticulously
to the lady in question
and matched to her trademark pillbox hat

Nor that it would be worn
on a crisp bluesky day in November
a day of parades and sunshine
a day of shaking hands
and heads
as the horizon disappeared
and compasses began to spin
in aimless circles
while earth's interior altered
tectonic plates shifted
and no one knew
what was going on
beneath the surface

That morning
the lady in the pink suit
whispered to the redhaired man
some small confidence
he laughed like a schoolboy
they held hands a moment
oblivious to photographers
then the long drive
the cheering crowds
they basked in the bliss
of being loved
by so many

Gunfire
everything shatters

A gash is torn
in heaven
the world hangs by a thread
spun by a spider
hidden among dusty textbooks
patiently waiting

Arthur slumps
blood and brain bloom
onto the pink suit
like some perverse corsage
and he is cradled
in soft wool
in her arms

Everything spins around her
the strand that anchors
as she waits at the hospital
as she hears him pronounced dead
as she stands strong
in the bloodstained suit

to see his unworthy successor
take the crown
Fifty years pass without answer
the blood has not dried
scars are unhealed
there is no solace

The lamb fell.

At the crossroads

Unleash the winds
and let the fire burn
incinerate the old year
in these limbs
scavenge memories
keep the good
let fall all sadness
to the forest floor
else standing on the edge
here at the crossroads
of the year, you yield
to slant rays of a dying sun
and peer into the abyss
let vertigo take you
weakened and wincing
from pain of old wounds
and you give in
when that old devil sidles up
and whispers in your ear:

Let slip the velvet cord
let drop the blade.

On defying the natural order

If the light
in autumn's final leaf
did not fall
or fade
or sink
to grief
but danced
into winter
a solitary wonder

refused to grace
the forest floor
leafmeal there
and nothing more
unwithered
daring everything
the deadly frost
the shock of cold
could shake the blight
and still burn gold
without a flicker

if that light
held strong and knew
another spring
its sap renewed
in every vein
and summer, too

o, for such hope
in such a light
that never dimmed

but dared the night
rebuked for all
the killing child
whose arrogance
would have it fall
and take its place

o, such a light
so dark an art
could topple
Eden's applecart.

Into this Eden

Let me not go down
into the earth that bore me
let not flesh sink
to alabaster bone
in silence
darkness
and alone

           Once within the Everglades
           dazzled by gilded reeds
           and dappled shade
           beneath a bright
           and cerulean sky
           I watched
           color and light
           conspire as friends
           to shift and part and suddenly
           reveal a golden panther
           in the splinter of a moment's end
           then saw it just as quickly fade
           to camouflage again

Let me go down so
myself disperse
meld into autumn light
merge and mingle
with shadows cast
by birds and dragonflies
let my words rise
a faint incense
upon the breeze
an almost-heard inflection

that sings hollow
rings of hope
within the sound
of water running softly underground
o let the meter that was mine
the living rhyme
that pumped my heart
and gave me life
and any worthy dream
I might have had
be one
with every glory burning bright
upon this earth

not high above
nor in between
nor yet below
but into this Eden
let me go
thus let me stay.

Dark lullaby

Just lately
this persistent rise and fall
of nonexistent cicada chorus
ringing in my ears
recalls how childhood evenings fell

how the sun abruptly dropped
below Old Farm Hill's crest
an exhausted orange ball
so done with day
how liliaceous morning skies
turned uncontrollably indigo
and like some small Neanderthal
I feared the sun would not return

how I put away playthings
and reluctant took
the once bright path
that downhill now
turned ominous and dark
deep with gathered shadows
mysterious with owls
and flap of wings invisible
heavy with howl
of Papa's old hunting dog
and fearsome hidden things

how with silver-fingered moon
insistent on my shoulders
I unwilling left
always wanting more
and feared the night and nothingness
of sleep

then once I cleared the crest
and started down
how the many-candled window
of Mama's house
grew bright against the dark
how fireflies lifted
tiny, ineffective lanterns
toward the stars
as ebb and rise of cicada
sang me home.

Solstice

Cain-whispered chant
binds us to limbic logic
pulses beneath clay and blood
beats the old war drum
provokes anger
we feed it
hate / bigotry / greed / envy
and it grows wintercold, heavy
anchors us
to the bottom
of the starless abyss

Otherwhere
star-speckled nightsky
wilderness gives life to promise
in a tangle of oak and holly
ripe fruit of prophecy
the holy daughter labors
not in vain
lying on damp straw
she bears redemption
second chances
as the New Sun dawns
that we too may rise
on radiant pinions
beyond ourselves.

Winter in the public gardens

The parking lot is empty
save for my car
and the old gardener
who rides his small cart
and checks on things
though he does nothing
to change them

One thing is clear
no one loves you in winter
when leaves have long abandoned
and limbs sunk down to barren bone
stretch long phalanges skyward
like supplicants imploring one more spring
while every greydawned morning
moves further from the light
and even birds have left this silent place

No one loves you
not the ones who planted you
and left without a thought
not sky-eyed children
who reveled in your cherryblossomed May
not the friendly photographers
whose careful calibrations captured summer
not even the old lovers
who watched autumn's firefall
drift flaming to the forest floor

I am here
at the end
brittle twig
sorrowful with icicles
I am here.

Snowblind

Bulbs I pocketed deep in fertile earth
disturb my sleep when snow falls
no matter how many times
I have seen them rise to trumpet spring

Cold has a way of shrinking faith to nothing
and even angels get vertigo
looking down on blinding fields
where every shining hope is lost in camouflage
they wait impatient for what hides beneath
to resurrect victorious

I suckle doubt tonight
cradle it in weak and human arms
and lay me down to somber dreams
uninterrupted by the shudder
of opalescent pinions
that hover invisible
and silent to fleshmuffled ears

Winter is my Gethsemane
dark and faithless passage
and if it yields a velvet-petaled crocus
perhaps, a February daffodil
Goddess-sent to make me out a liar
when morning sun illuminates again
this cross is worth the bearing.

Matin

Oh how I love that sacred hour
beneath the glowering grey
worry thorn-pressed on my brow
feeling that nothing can change

and when the heavy anguish
of life, of age, of death
with all its sorrows
seems beyond bearing
dawn ambushes me
slips stealthy from behind
and of a sudden, trees
are all alight before me
damp bark nearly incandescent
birds waken singing
and I know morning is
a woman on rampage
cleaning house
making things right
graceful alchemist
transforming
bruised and blackened limbs
to flaming glory
transmuting
skies pewter
to aquamarine

and I know how good it is
to find ourselves
facing away from the light
sometimes
to know the dizzying depths
of the abyss

for an hour terrible and divine
to tremble on the edge
to fear the night eternal
then see it vanquished
by this unmerited surprise
that changes everything

it's not the morning light
I treasure so
it is the darkness
makes the dawn so dear.

The child who can believe

I want to be the child who can believe
and never watch the wonder die away
into the faded dawn of a graceless day

I want to be the child who always sees
the fairy in the dragonfly's disguise
the beauty in the beast that men despise

I want to be the child who still has faith
in Christmas night and early Easter morn
the triumph of the rose above the thorn

You may keep your science black and white
hypotheses, experiments alike
let reason give you comfort in the night

But leave to me the legend and the lore
and I will shelter them within my heart
that miracle and myth shall not depart

And I shall find my comfort in the word
that echoes down millennia to remind
that truth is in the heart and not the mind

I'll follow close that other child who leads
down twisted paths where only faith can go
to glories only innocence can know

I want to be the child who can believe
and never watch the wonder die away
into the faded dawn of a graceless day.

Pockets

He wore a coat with many pockets
one held the gore and smoke of battlefields
another a meadow
where poppies burned scarlet
amongst gilded wheat

It was a coat with many pockets
one muffled the cries of children
lovers hidden away in one
and in another
there was straw
a feeding trough
and a lot of good intentions

There were many pockets
one for babies orphaned or abandoned
another concealed barren women
several held broken promises
questions without answers
the futility of pain

How heavy, these many pockets
one bulged with forgotten gardens
seeds unplanted
oil-slicked waters
and air that corrodes

So many pockets
bloody altars in one
a crucifix rusted in another
there was a rosary strung with Stars of David
crescent moons and a pentagram
manmade stories

that lost more meaning
with every telling

A coat with many pockets
enough for the whole world
one for sins
another for good deeds
now that I remember
he stood a bit lop-sided

Burdened by so many pockets
with prayers and sunsets
and first stars rising
on nameless hopes

There were so many pockets
the addicted and estranged
empty hands of the hungry
the hollow-eyed homeless
with only this small pocket
for shelter

There were these many pockets
one for me
that I kept falling out of
climbing back up
by fraying threads
then sliding back down
as he trudged on
dragging the great coat behind him

So many pockets
left to fill.

Credo

Energy cannot be created or destroyed; it can only be changed from one form to another. – Albert Einstein

I cannot believe
in these small and evenhours
as light dwindles down
to purple shades and grey
and winter tucks away these sleeping flowers
beneath a silent comforter of snow
that we are alone in this
or meaningless

as trees stand skeletal
and bared to silvered bone
I understand
that earth alone is not a sphere
but all things here
the spiral journey bear
I know what slumbers
know what lies beneath
this frigid earth, what dreams of April birth
and even science can't deny
energy does not die
neither, then, shall I

whatever waiting room
I occupy in afterwhere
when ash has scattered
and is one with all
I shall not disappear
but hold it as self-evident
that daffodils gone down
will rise eventually
that birds return
and butterflies
and me.

Out of the bonecage singing

Out of the bonecage singing, singing
sprung free at last
once clipped prisoner
mounting skyward on early wings
into the dawning afterwhere
earth's minion, Eden lover
on shining pinions soaring
into the airy kingdom
riding winds of morning
rising into the holy
flight upward
wholly sunward
skydance to old rhythms
long forgotten music
fleshmuffled in the otherwhere
now remembered
in spirit's beforeplace
far beneath, one glory
high above, another
horizon now level
now full tilt
sunrays crepuscular
lightward quickened
flights of angels
rush to welcome.

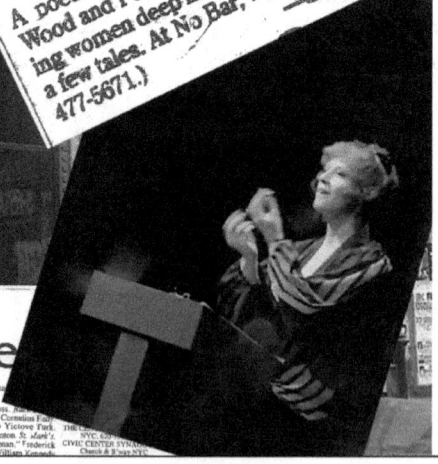

About the Poet

Carla Martin-Wood has been a widely published poet since 1978. Recently retired from her career in the rat race world of advertising, she is relishing her newfound freedom.

The author of five full-length books of poetry, Carla's most recent collection is *Stories from Eden* (The Pink Petticoat Press, 2012). She has also authored eight chapbooks, most recently *Season of Mists* (The 99% Press, 2012).

A copy of Carla's chapbook, *Garden of Regret* (Pudding House Publications Chapbook Series, 2009), resides in the Special Collections & University Archives at Stanford University, contributed by the renowned Russian poet, essayist and dramatist, Yevgeny Yevtushenko.

Carla's poems have appeared in a plethora of journals and numerous anthologies in the US, England, and Ireland since 1978. With a background of 13 years in theatre, she has performed her work from the hallowed University of The South at Sewanee to legendary Greenwich Village.

She has been nominated for The Pushcart Prize a dozen times, for Best of the Net twice, and is listed in Poets & Writers.

A lifelong political and social activist, Carla's introduction to activism was as one of four white teens who fought their way through picket lines to break the white boycott of a high school in Birmingham, Alabama during the violent racial conflicts of 1963. She continued as an activist for human rights, the anti-war movement and NOW through the 1980s. Her current interests lie in preservation of the earth, universal healthcare and gun control.

Acknowledgements

Dark lullaby was nominated for The Pushcart Prize 2011 by The Pink Petticoat Press

Into this Eden was nominated for The Pushcart Prize 2012 by The 99% Press

Dark lullaby and Witness appeared in *Into the Windfall Light* (The Pink Petticoat Press, 2012)

Into this Eden, October song and *Plea to autumn* appeared in *Season of Mists* (The 99% Press, 2012)

The child who can believe first appeared in *The Lyric*

Love in the space-time continuum, The diagnosis, and *Legacy* first appeared in *Ariadne's Thread*

Pockets and *Love song for my brother* first appeared in *The Tower Poetry Journal*

Also by this author

Season of Mists
The 99% Press

Stories from Eden
The Pink Petticoat Press

How we are loved
Fortunate Childe Publications

Into the Windfall Light
The Pink Petticoat Press

Flight Risk & Other Poems
Fortunate Childe Publications

One flew east
Fortunate Childe Publications

Songs from the Web
Fortunate Childe Publications

Absinthe & Valentines
Flutter Press

The Last Magick
Fortunate Childe Publications

HerStory
Fortunate Childe Publications

Feed Sack Majesty
Fortunate Childe Publications

Redheaded Stepchild
Pudding House Chapbook Series

Garden of Regret
Pudding House Chapbook Series

out of the bonecage singing

carla martin-wood

www.ingramcontent.com/pod-product-compliance
Lightning Source LLC
Chambersburg PA
CBHW062024040426
42447CB00010B/2132